D0966442

# LEARNING ABOUT THE EARTH

# Mountains

by Emily K. Green

BLASTOFF!
3
READERS

BELLWETHER MEDIA · MINNEAPOLIS, MN

Note to Librarians, Teachers, and Parents:

**Blastoff! Readers** are carefully developed by literacy experts and combine standards-based content with developmentally appropriate text.

**Level 1** provides the most support through repetition of high-frequency words, light text, predictable sentence patterns, and strong visual support.

**Level 2** offers early readers a bit more challenge through varied simple sentences, increased text load, and less repetition of high-frequency words.

**Level 3** advances early-fluent readers toward fluency through increased text and concept load, less reliance on visuals, longer sentences, and more literary language.

**Level 4** builds reading stamina by providing more text per page, increased use of punctuation, greater variation in sentence patterns, and increasingly challenging vocabulary.

**Level 5** encourages children to move from "learning to read" to "reading to learn" by providing even more text, varied writing styles, and less familiar topics.

Whichever book is right for your reader, Blastoff! Readers are the perfect books to build confidence and encourage a love of reading that will last a lifetime!

This edition first published in 2011 by Bellwether Media, Inc.

No part of this publication may be reproduced in whole or in part without written permission of the publisher. For information regarding permission, write to Bellwether Media, Inc., Attention: Permissions Department, 5357 Penn Avenue South, Minneapolis, MN 55419.

Library of Congress Cataloging-in-Publication Data
Green, Emily K., 1966-
  Mountains / by Emily K. Green.
    p. cm. — (Blastoff! readers) (Learning about the Earth)
  Summary: "Simple text and supportive images introduce beginning readers to the physical characteristics and geographic locations of mountains."
  Includes bibliographical references and index.
  ISBN 978-0-531-26031-9 (paperback : alk. paper)
  1. Mountains—Juvenile literature. I. Title. II. Series.
  GB512.G75 2007
  551.43'2—dc22
                                        2006000571

Printed in the United States of America.      010111      1185

# Table of Contents

Mountains are high places on
the earth. A mountain is taller
than the land all around it.

A mountain can even rise
above the **clouds.**

5

Mountains are made of rock.

Some mountains are rounded and smooth.

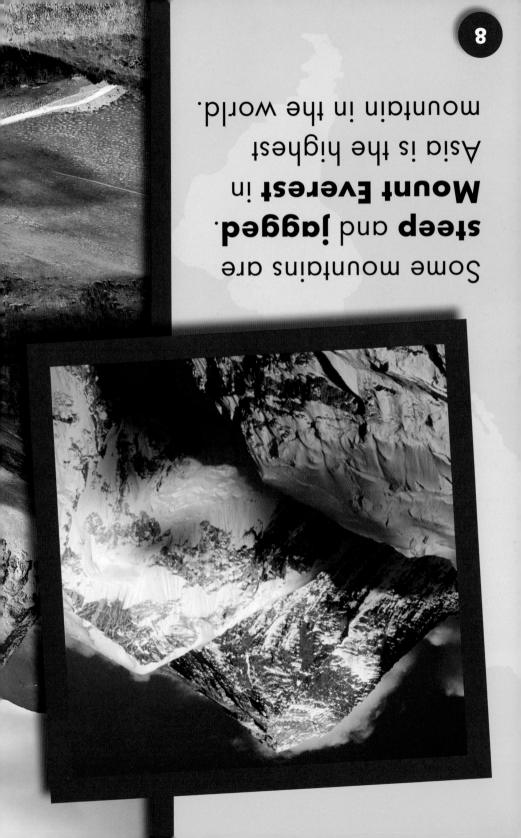

Some mountains are **steep** and **jagged**. **Mount Everest** in Asia is the highest mountain in the world.

Most mountains sit in a line or a group called a **range**.

Some mountains rise
from the bottom of
the ocean.

Some underwater mountains are tall enough to break through the surface. These mountains make **islands**.

The top of a mountain is called the **peak**. The air is always colder at the peak.

The peaks of high
mountains may be
covered in snow
and ice all year.

The sides of a mountain are called **slopes.**

Plants and trees may grow
on the slopes.

Many rivers begin in the mountains. Melted snow flows down the slopes of mountains. The water flows into streams.

The streams flow into rivers.

Rocks on a mountain sometimes crack and break loose. Falling rock is called an **avalanche**.

Snow can make
avalanches, too.

Some people like to **climb** mountains. People need special **equipment** to climb the highest mountains.

Other people like to
go down mountains.
Whooosh!

# Glossary

**avalanche**—rock or snow falling down a mountain

**climb**—to go up

**clouds**—a clump of water drops and dust in the sky

**equipment**—gear used for a specific activity

**island**—area of land surrounded by water on all sides

**jagged**—sharp and rocky

**Mount Everest**—the highest mountain on Earth; Mount Everest sits on the border of Nepal and China.

**peak**—the top of a mountain

**range**—a line or group of mountains

**slopes**—the sides of a mountain

**steep**—slopes that go up very quickly

# To Learn More

## AT THE LIBRARY

Huneck, Stephen. *Sally Goes to the Mountains*. New York: Harry N. Abrams, 2001.

Lawson, Julie. *Midnight in the Mountains*. Custer, Wash.: Orca, 1998.

Lobel, Arnold. *Ming Lo Moves the Mountain*. New York: HarperCollins Inc., 1993.

Locker, Thomas. *Mountain Dance*. San Diego: Silver Whistle/Harcourt, 2001.

McLerran, Alice. *The Mountain That Loved a Bird*. Riverside, NJ: Simon & Schuster, Inc., 1985.

## ON THE WEB

Learning more about mountains is as easy as 1, 2, 3.

1. Go to www.factsurfer.com

2. Enter "mountains" into search box.

3. Click the "Surf" button and you will see a list of related web sites.

With factsurfer.com, finding more information is just a click away.

# Index

The photographs in this book are reproduced through the courtesy of: Joseph Van Os/Getty Images, front cover; Harvey Lloyd/Getty Images, pp. 4-5; G Brad Lewis/Getty Images, p. 6; Greg Pease/Getty Images, p. 7; Richard l'Anson/Getty Images, p. 8; Alan Kearney/Getty Images, pp. 9, 18; Art Wolfe/Getty Images, pp. 10-11; Ed Darack/Getty Images, pp. 12-13; Grant Dixon/Getty Images, p. 13; Bill Hatcher/Getty Images, p. 14; Orion Press/Getty Images, p. 15; Photolibrarycom/Getty Images, p. 16; Matthias Clamer/Getty Images, p. 17; Tim Laman/Getty Images, p. 19; Jake Norton/Getty Images, p. 20; Tim Barnett/Getty Images, p. 21.